Irving Berlin
The Immigrant Boy Who Made America Sing

By Nancy Churnin
Illustrated by James Rey Sanchez

Creston Books

Irving stood on tiptoe to see over the rail. Behind him, too far to glimpse, was Russia where angry Cossacks had burned his family's home to ashes. Ahead was America. What would they find there?

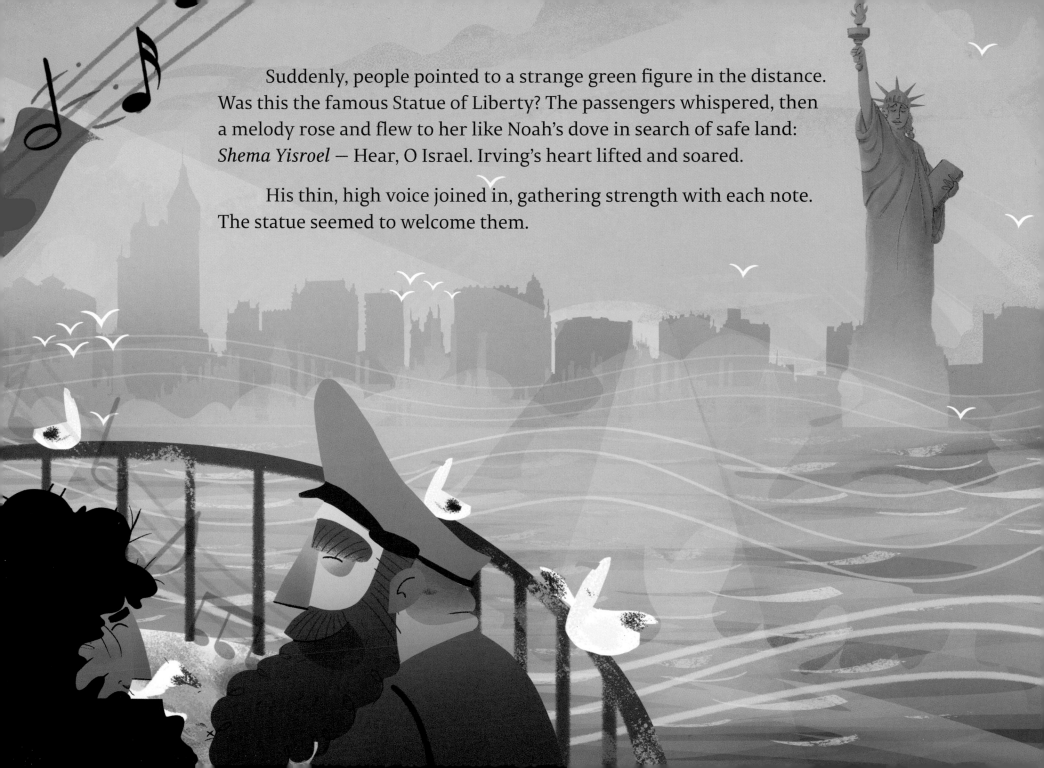

Suddenly, people pointed to a strange green figure in the distance. Was this the famous Statue of Liberty? The passengers whispered, then a melody rose and flew to her like Noah's dove in search of safe land: *Shema Yisroel* — Hear, O Israel. Irving's heart lifted and soared.

His thin, high voice joined in, gathering strength with each note. The statue seemed to welcome them.

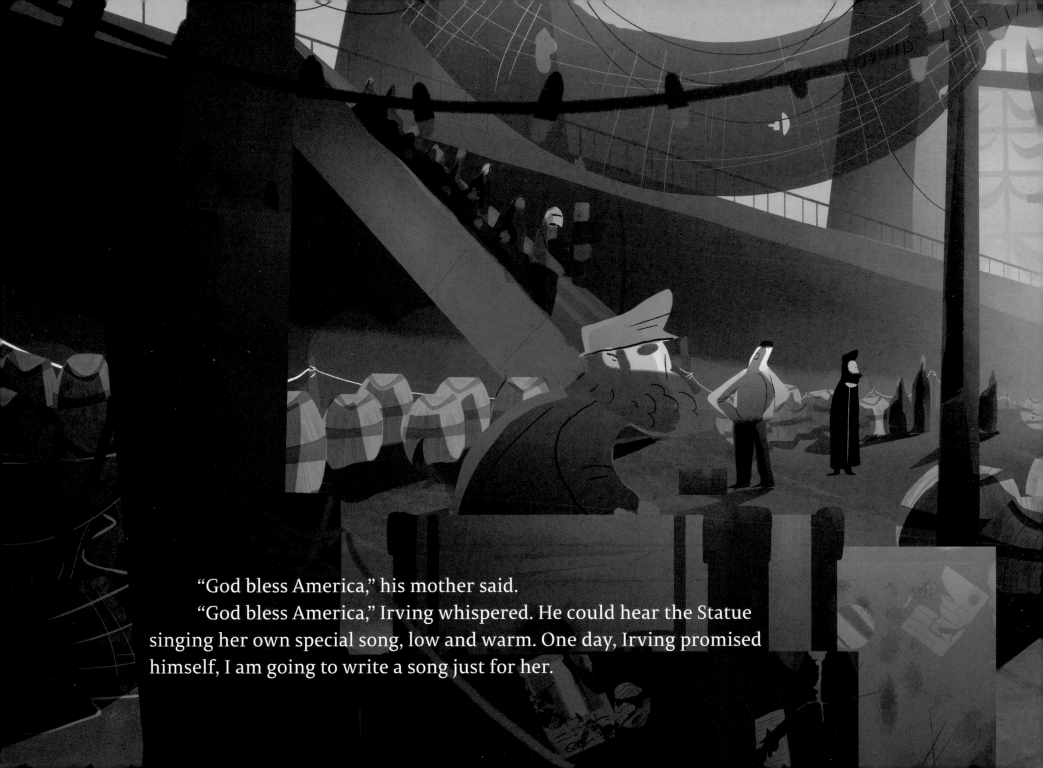

"God bless America," his mother said.

"God bless America," Irving whispered. He could hear the Statue singing her own special song, low and warm. One day, Irving promised himself, I am going to write a song just for her.

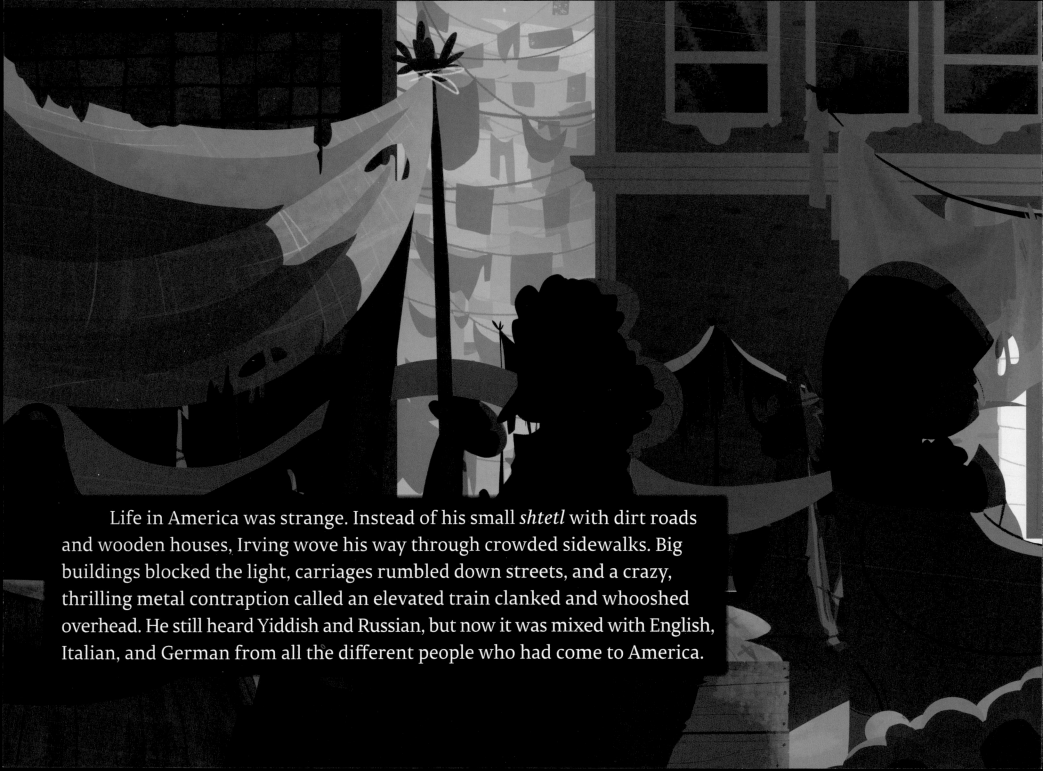

Life in America was strange. Instead of his small *shtetl* with dirt roads and wooden houses, Irving wove his way through crowded sidewalks. Big buildings blocked the light, carriages rumbled down streets, and a crazy, thrilling metal contraption called an elevated train clanked and whooshed overhead. He still heard Yiddish and Russian, but now it was mixed with English, Italian, and German from all the different people who had come to America.

Music was everywhere. Irving sang in the synagogue with his father, who had been a cantor in Russia, the one whose voice carried people's prayers to the heavens. Walking home, the melodies in his head mixed with the crack of stickball games, the wail of the ragmen, and the creak of cartwheels on the cobblestones.

Back in his family's crowded apartment, there were more sounds. The steady treadle of the sewing machine in the apartment next door. The thump of his mother kneading dough, and soft laughter when his father pressed his cheek against her floury face. Irving lay awake, late at night, trying to fit all the notes and words together.

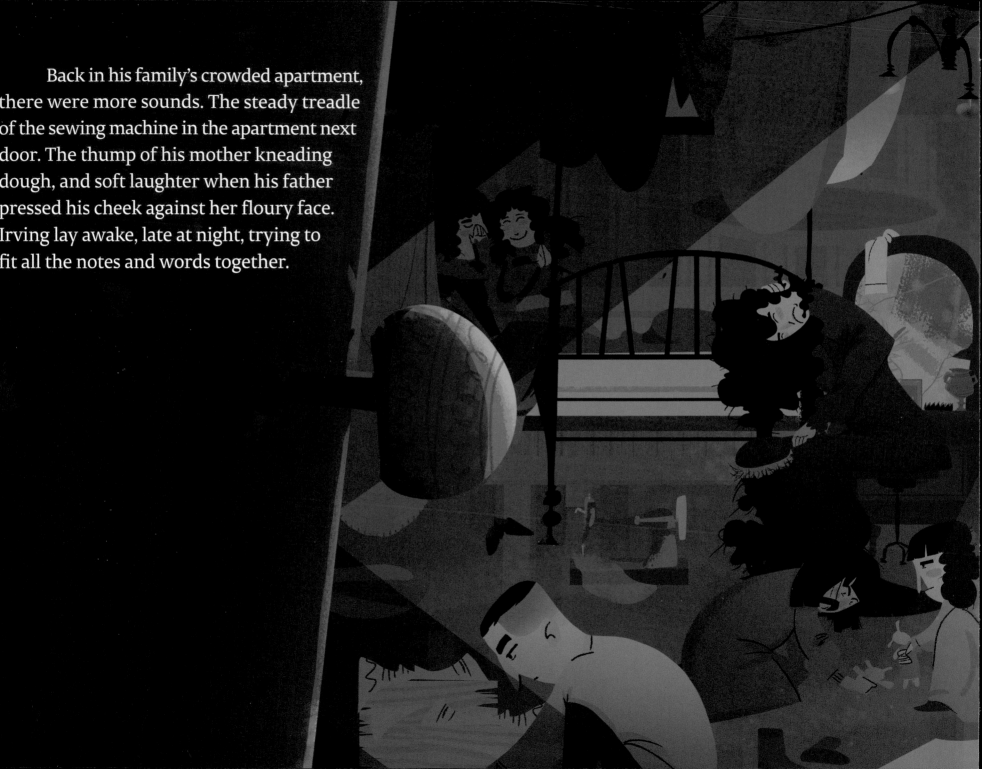

When Irving was 13, his father died. Still a boy, Irving quit school to sell newspapers, earning pennies to help feed his family. Ashamed of being another mouth to feed, he scrounged scraps and slept in a dirty tenement with hundreds of other ragged, homeless kids.

Even there, he was always listening. Snatches of jazz, bits of lullabies, whispered jokes. One day, while he was selling papers, he couldn't stop the notes swirling in his head. He burst out singing. People stopped, smiled, and tossed him coins.

Irving stared at the bits of copper glinting in the sun. People were paying him for music? Would they do it again?

He tried singing popular songs on street corners. Irving didn't have the strongest voice, but his hummable melodies and catchy rhymes made people smile and stick around for more.

People threw enough coins that a passing restaurant owner noticed and offered Irving a job as a singing waiter. A real job, making music!

Irving wanted to write the melodies he heard in his head and felt in his heart, but he didn't know how. So every day after the restaurant emptied, he slowly tried to pick out tunes on the old piano.

At first he was terrible, but slowly he got better. People noticed. When a singer at another restaurant wrote a hit song, Irving's boss asked him to do the same thing. Irving still didn't know how to write down music, but the restaurant's pianist did. He helped Irving write "Marie from Sunny Italy." They sold it for 37 cents. At 19, Irving was a paid songwriter!

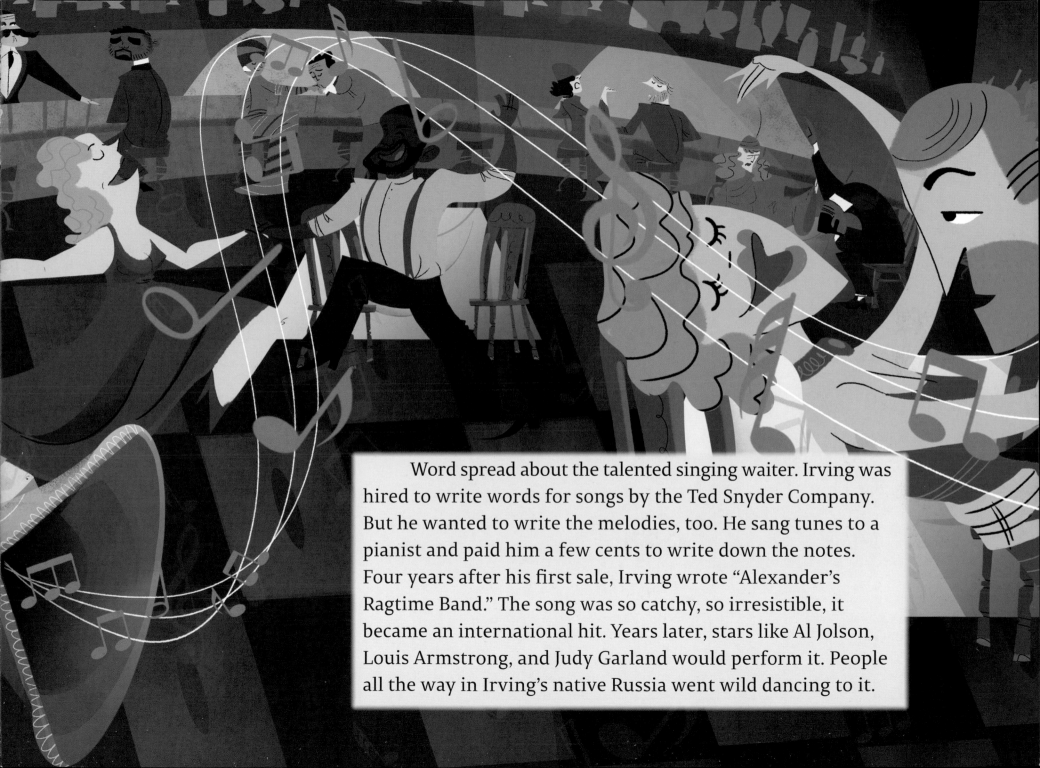

Word spread about the talented singing waiter. Irving was hired to write words for songs by the Ted Snyder Company. But he wanted to write the melodies, too. He sang tunes to a pianist and paid him a few cents to write down the notes. Four years after his first sale, Irving wrote "Alexander's Ragtime Band." The song was so catchy, so irresistible, it became an international hit. Years later, stars like Al Jolson, Louis Armstrong, and Judy Garland would perform it. People all the way in Irving's native Russia went wild dancing to it.

Irving wasn't a waiter anymore. His songs made a lot more than pennies. Now he and his family were never hungry or worried about how to pay rent. But even after he moved to a fancy apartment, Irving would walk a few blocks to his old neighborhood in the Bowery where he could listen to the rhythms of the street, the sounds that would fill his music.

When the United States entered World War I, the Army put Irving to work writing patriotic songs. He wrote an entire Broadway musical for the soldiers called *Yip! Yip! Yaphank!* His mother watched proudly, wishing his father could hear the applause, as Sergeant Berlin sang "Oh! How I Hate To Get Up in the Morning." Every night the audience roared as Irving and the 300-person cast marched down the aisles and out the door, singing the final song, "We're on Our Way to France." On closing night, the soldiers marched out the door and onto the troop carrier which took most of them to France — for real.

Twenty years later, when the United States was getting ready to enter World War II, Irving wanted to help his country again. He picked up a song that he'd originally written for the WWI show finale but never used. It ended with three notes from the *Shema,* as he remembered hearing them on the boat, coming to America, long ago when the Statue had smiled at his prayer. He blended the melody with his mother's words: "God Bless America." At the end of the old melody, he added new words about the land he loved. Irving showed the song to his friend, Kate Smith, the famous singer. Would she understand what he was trying to say?

Kate hummed the notes, read the words, and nodded.

From the mountains, to the prairies,
to the oceans white with foam, Americans all over the
country huddled around their radios, listening to Kate Smith
sing "God Bless America." On the eve of the dark days of WWII,
the song filled them with hope and courage.

It still fills people with hope and courage.

Over the years, Irving earned a lot of money from songs like "Always," "There's No Business Like Show Business," and "White Christmas." But he never took a penny for "God Bless America."

Irving gave everything the song earned, millions of dollars, to children in the Girl and Boy Scouts. It was his thank you to the country that opened its arms to countless people from all over the world, including a homeless boy who came to America with nothing but music in his heart.

Author's Note

Irving Berlin was born May 11, 1888 as Israel Baline in Western Siberia in Russia. He was five when he immigrated with his family to the United States.

Irving loved music, but never had lessons. When he got a job as a singing waiter at 18, he taught himself how to play the piano, but only mastered one key, F-sharp. In 1909, he saved up to buy a transposing upright piano for $100 that allowed him to change keys by pulling or pushing a lever.

He used the piano to compose his first big hit, "Alexander's Ragtime Band" in 1911 and later for another hit, "I Love a Piano," in 1915.

Irving wrote more than 1,500 songs, including scores for 19 Broadway shows and 18 movies. Among his songs: "White Christmas," "Easter Parade," "Cheek to Cheek,"and "Always," which became a hit for Patsy Cline, "Blue Skies," a 1927 success that became a hit again for Willie Nelson in 1978, "Puttin' on the Ritz," a song featured in the Mel Brooks' film and Broadway hit *Young Frankenstein,* and the score for Broadway's *Annie Get Your Gun*, which includes the Broadway and Hollywood favorite, "There's No Business Like Show Business."

Irving's first wife, Dorothy Goetz, a singer, died of typhoid fever not long after they married in 1912. He wrote his first ballad, called "When I Lost You," for her. In 1926, he married Ellin McKay. Ellin's father objected to Irving because he was Jewish and their family was Catholic, but the marriage lasted 62 years until her death in July 1988 at age 85.

The couple had three daughters and one son, Irving Berlin Jr., who died on Christmas Day at three weeks old. Irving would say *kaddish,* the Jewish prayer for the dead, and visit his son's grave every Christmas. He also was known to throw pennies to neighborhood children (no doubt remembering what receiving pennies meant to him as a child) and then celebrate Christmas with his wife and daughters.

Songwriters make their money from royalties — money that people pay each time they perform a song professionally. Irving made a lot of money from his songs over the years, but he gave all of the vast royalties for his patriotic masterpieces, "God Bless America" to the Girl and Boy Scouts of America, and for *This is the Army* to the Army Emergency Relief Fund, which earned millions of dollars for these organizations.

"God Bless America" was an immediate hit when Kate Smith sang it on the CBS Radio Program at the New York World's Fair on Nov. 10, Armistice Day, which is now known as Veteran's Day. It continues to be popular at baseball games, where it has been played during the seventh inning stretch ever since the Sept. 11, 2001 terrorist attacks.

Irving died Sept. 22, 1989 at age 101, 10 months after Ellin died, in New York City. Over the years, fans used to gather outside his home on Christmas to sing "White Christmas." After he died, people gathered outside his home and sang "God Bless America" in his memory.

I want to thank the Berlin family and Ted Chapin, of the Irving Berlin Music Company, for their kindness in fact-checking and supporting the manuscript. I am also profoundly grateful to Mark Kreditor, an inspiring music educator, pianist, and composer, who has generously shared his insights about the connections between Irving Berlin's music and the cantorial tradition.